GROSS AND Frightening ANIMAL FACTS

Stinky ANIMALS

Stella Tarakson

MASON CREST

THAT'S STINKY!

Mason Crest
450 Parkway Drive, Suite D
Broomall, Pennsylvania 19008
(866) MCP-BOOK (toll free)

First printing
9 8 7 6 5 4 3 2 1

ISBN (hardback) 978-1-4222-3929-2
ISBN (series) 978-1-4222-3923-0
ISBN (ebook) 978-1-4222-7866-6

Cataloging-in-Publication Data on file with the Library of Congress

Lethal Animals
Text copyright © 2015 Pascal Press Written by Stella Tarakson

First published 2015 by Pascal Press PO Box 250, Glebe, NSW 2037 Australia

Publisher: Lynn Dickinson Principal Photographer: Steve Parish © Nature-Connect Pty Ltd
Additional Photography: See p. 48 Researcher: Clare Thomson, Wild Card Media Editor: Vanessa Barker

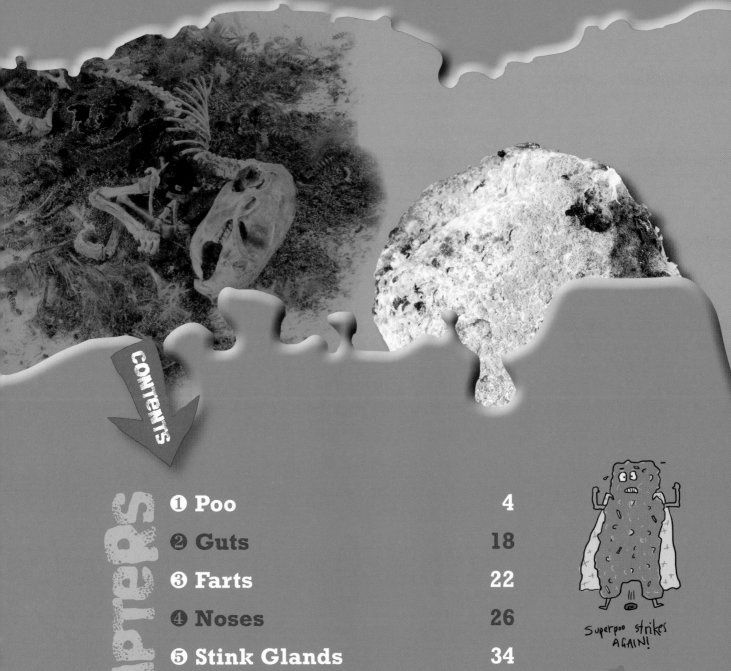

Superpoo strikes AGAIN!

THAT'S STINKY!

CHAPTER 1

Poo

Poo, crap, stools, excrement—there are many names for feces, and some are nastier than others. But there's one thing everyone agrees on—poo stinks! There's a reason for that, apart from just to gross you out. It's to stop people eating it! The smell of poo comes from bacteria in the stomach and intestines. Poo harbors harmful germs, such as E. coli. You don't want that anywhere near your lunch!

SUPER POOPER SCOOPER

Whale scientists use giant scoopers to collect whale poo from the surface of the ocean. Why? So they can examine it to discover what the whales have been eating.

THE POO DICTIONARY

Copro	= dung
Scatology	= the study of poo
Coprolite	= fossilized poo
Coprophage	= poo eater
Coprophile	= poo lover

SEA SICK

Did you know cat poo can make dolphins sick? Feline poo contains resilient parasites called oocysts. Dolphins can become infected when the poo get washed down drains and into the sea.

LET'S STINK TOGETHER

Bats stick together ... and poo together. The droppings left by a whole cave full of bats can make a huge pile! Scientists can discover what bats were eating in the distant past by collecting and analyzing fossilized bat poo. That's one mountain you wouldn't want to climb!

LIFE INSIDE A POO

I'M JUST A POO...

LET ME OUT OF HERE!

There was an old woman who lived in a poo ... no, that's not right! But there are two types of mallee moths that do. As caterpillars, they make their home in koala excrement. They feed on the poo and then line the insides of their hollowed-out homes with silk. Their own waste is ejected through small openings in the koala kaka.

THE POO BUS

When plants want to spread their seeds around, who do they call? The cassowary poo bus! When the cassowary goes for a walk and defecates, the seeds of fruit it has eaten are "dropped off" in new areas. Cassowaries are big birds, so they can carry the seeds of more than 70 species of large-fruiting trees that other smaller animals can't eat.

ALL ABOARD!

THAT WAS AN INTERESTING RIDE!

A CRAPPY DISGUISE

Some spiders have evolved cunning disguises to protect them from predators. But how about poo camouflage? The celaenia spider is also known as the bird-dropping spider for its unappetizing disguise.

I'M A LITTLE POO.

A POO POO PLATTER!

Sulphur-crested cockatoos love sifting through cow pies for undigested seeds the cows have eaten. Talk about bird breath!

toilet paper cape!

JUST WHEN YOU THOUGHT EVERYTHING WAS DONE... ALONG COMES SUPERPOO!

POO PACKAGE

The chicks of some birds, such as wrens, make it easy for their parents to keep the nest clean. They produce a little mucus-membrane-covered package called a fecal sac, which contains their poo inside. Their parents can simply pick it up and throw it away— but some even eat it!

How can you track down where different animals live? By looking out for their droppings! Scientists can learn a lot about an animal's diet and behavior by studying its poo. Seeds, pieces of bone and undigested material can tell researchers what the animals have been eating.

This also goes for the echidna, whose poo often glitters with shiny, undigested insect exoskeletons! An echidna doesn't have teeth, so it has to grind its prey between its tongue and the bottom of its mouth. Its stomach lining grinds the contents further before they enter the small intestine. Eventually it all comes out as a cylinder-shaped poo known as scat.

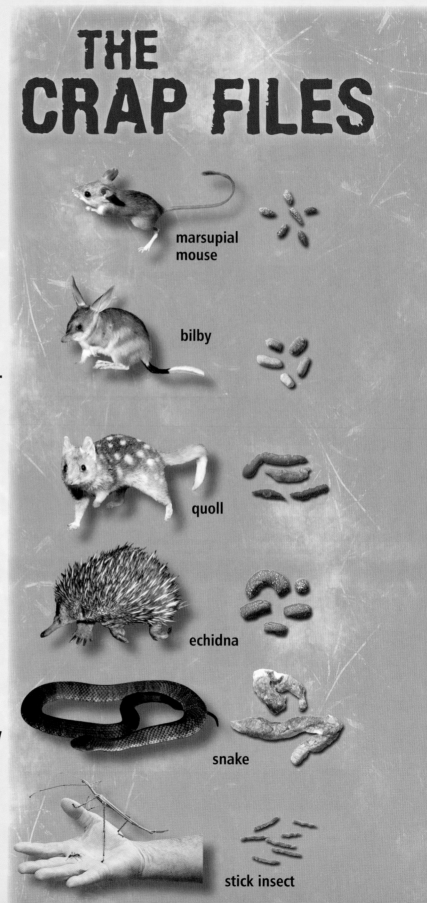

THE CRAP FILES

marsupial mouse

bilby

quoll

echidna

snake

stick insect

WHIFFY FIELD GUIDE

What animal did that poo come from? Next time you're out and about, you'll be able to impress your friends!

wombat

dingo

kangaroo

Superpoo strikes AGAIN!

LOOK TWICE

Not everything that looks like poo is poo! Many bird species spew out pellets or lumps of indigestible leftovers. Although they look like droppings, they are actually made of bits of food trapped and crushed in the gizzard. These can also be analyzed to determine a bird's diet.

FULL OF IT

Some big snakes, such as boas and vipers, can be constipated for over a year! This sometimes worries people who keep them as pets. But the snakes don't have tummy trouble. They use their heavy poo to help them keep their balance!

TOO MUCH EFFORT

Three-toed sloths are notoriously lazy. They spend most of their time sleeping and eating while hanging around in trees. They rarely descend to the ground—and if they do, it's usually just to go to the bathroom! And even then, it's only once every week or two!

LET IT BREW...

FOLLOW THE TRAIL

The New Zealand takahe bird poos every ten minutes! Laid out end-to-end, that's 26 feet (8 meters) of dung per day!

NO CAN POO

Did you know that microscopic mites live at the base of your eyebrows and eyelashes? Luckily the hair follicle mite has no anus, so it can't poo. But that means all the waste builds up. The mite lives for 2-3 weeks—then it explodes!

YUM FROM THE BUM

Koala joeys can't digest gum leaves themselves. They eat soft gum leaf poo to get the bacteria they need—straight from their mother's bottom!

BROWNIES FOR BREAKFAST AGAIN?

A fossilized cockroach from the dinosaur age was found to contain wood particles. The wood was partially digested, but cockroaches of that time weren't able to do that. Something else had eaten the wood first. The conclusion? The cockroach had lunched on dinosaur poo!

DINNER IS SERVED!

Rabbits and other small herbivores make a meal out of their own poo! It allows them to digest food further, so they get more nutrients the second time around.

VAMPIRE SQUID FROM HELL

Any poo will do! That's the motto of the vampire squid, which feasts on any fecal matter it comes across. They're the only cephalopod (carnivorous marine mollusc) not to hunt living prey. *Vampyroteuthis infernalis*, or the "vampire squid from hell," has an unusual way of eating. It has a pair of thin, retractable filaments that float free like a fishing line. The filaments pick up waste as they drift. The squid then mixes the waste with mucus that it secretes from its suckers, forming blobs of food that it then eats.

GIVE ME FECES ANY DAY!

BEAUTY TIPS

The bright yellow face of the Egyptian vulture is irresistible to its mate. To keep its features vibrant, the vulture gorges on cow, sheep and goat poo! These are rich in carotenoids—organic pigments found in plants and bacteria. Fortunately, we humans can get carotenoids from fruit and vegetables!

DROWNING IN IT

BETTER OUT THAN IN!

Cows in Australia produce so much dung that native poo-eating insects can't handle it! The average cow drops 10–12 huge, steaming cow pies per day. A few decades ago the problem was growing out of hand, with cow pies smothering pastures. In 1970, a scientist had a smart idea. He introduced dung beetles from Europe—and they quickly got to work recycling the waste!

A steaming vat of cow poo—gardeners are coprophiles, using manure as fertilizer to help their plants grow.

MISSION TURD BUSTER

They're on a mission—troops of dung beetles flying about on the lookout for a nice, juicy poo! Dung beetles have an incredible sense of smell. Their large antennae are covered with thousands of small hairs, called sensilla, which can actually sniff out poo. Once a target is detected, it's time to attack!

DUNG AND DUSTED

Imagine if your food were bigger than you. Then imagine that food is poo! Dung beetles chew off big chunks of dung and roll it away. They have to move quickly, or rivals might try to steal their food. When they reach a safe distance away, they dig a tunnel in the soil and roll the dung ball into it. The balls are then either eaten or eggs are laid inside them.

FUSSY EATERS

A council in Sydney, Australia has released dung beetles to clean up dog feces in streets and parks. Now that's community service!

YOU POO TOO

Everybody does it, even if we don't like to talk about it! The average person creates about 9 ounces (250 grams) of poo per day. When you multiply that by the number of people on the planet (7.28 billion and counting), that's a serious load of crap! Fortunately, sewage is handled efficiently in many places of the developed world. Only a few hundred years ago, even people in wealthy countries simply tossed their turds into the streets!

I AM READY TO GO!

The toilet invasion

People who live in the Australian tropics need to check their toilets before they sit—there might be a frog inside! As bizarre as it sounds, green tree-frogs like to make toilets their homes. They don't drink the loo water, absorbing it through their skin instead.

Just like humans, frogs need to go before a long trip. They can jump farther with an empty bladder!

A SOCIAL EVENT

SEE YOU AT TWO!

Quolls like to socialize as they do the deed. They don't just share gossip— they also share communal bush toilet sites! Located in open spaces, each one has a big pile of droppings that gets bigger with time.

PARROTFISH PARATROOPERS

Parrotfish are very fussy about where they poo, and they all use the same spot. Once the location has been decided, each fish passes over it and and lets one go. It can take just four days to build up 66 pounds (30 kilograms) of parrotfish poo!

BOMBS AWAY!

CHAPTER 2

GUTS

Why do people say "I hate your guts"? They've never seen your guts! And if they did, surely they'd be impressed! Although intestines are coiled tightly within our abdomens, they are amazingly long.

HUMANS

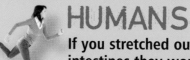

If you stretched out a human's intestines they would be 30 feet (9 meters) long—that's more than four times our body length!

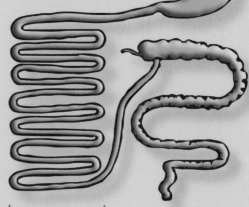

1 foot (30 cm)

BIRDS

0.8 inch (2 cm)

Birds have gizzards, a muscular pouch in the lower stomach. A gizzard works a bit like a pepper grinder. It contains grit, helping the food break down into pieces small enough to be digested.

WHALES

8 inches (20 cm)

The length of a human's intestines is nothing compared to a sperm whale's intestines. They are 177 feet (54 meters) long—that's more than the length of an Olympic-sized swimming pool!

KOALAS

The koala is one of the few mammals that can live off gum leaves, which are poisonous to most other animals. The leaves are very fibrous and hard to digest. Koalas ferment them in a part of their gut called the caecum. It is filled with bacteria that break down the food. Koalas have a bigger caecum than any other animal and can eat 1 pound (half a kilo) of gum leaves a day!

4 inches (10 cm)

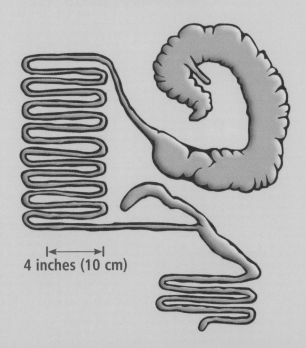

KANGAROOS

Kangaroos eat great quantities of fibrous plants like grasses. They have chambered stomachs similar to sheep and cattle. A kangaroo's large forestomach is filled with bacteria that ferment the plant material into fatty acids, which are then absorbed into the bloodstream.

4 inches (10 cm)

BRAINY GUTS

Did you know you have two brains? The human gut has been called our second brain because it has an estimated 500 million nerve cells. A rat's brain only has about 100 million nerve cells!

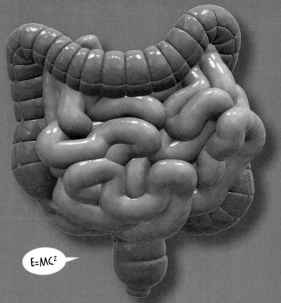

E=MC²

are you serious?

The flatworm uses the same hole as a mouth and a bottom!

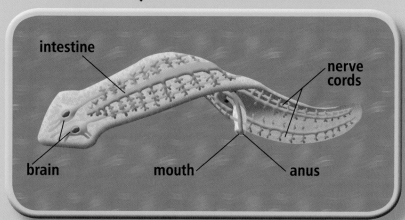

intestine

nerve cords

brain   mouth   anus

YOU SHOULD SEE WHAT COMES OUT OF HIS MOUTH!

I EAT DIRT

An earthworm eats by turning its throat inside out through its mouth. It picks up dirt and swallows it by drawing it back into its body. Once the earthworm has digested all the nutrients, it excretes a mass of dirt called a cast out its other end.

What a good idea

Apart from sounding appetizing, sea gooseberries and sea walnuts are also ahead of the pack when it comes to digestion. They were some of the first animals to evolve a digestive canal that had a mouth at one end and an anus at the other!

BOTTOM BAG

Diadem urchins appear to be built upside down! Their mouths are on their undersides and their anuses are on top, with an anal sac to store their poo. Because of this, they need to take particular care when defecating. Their poo is shot out with considerable force to stop it from dirtying their spines!

THE HUMAN URCHIN

CHAPTER 3

FARTS

Flatulence—better known as farts—is air or gas in the stomach or intestines. It's caused by bacteria breaking down partially digested food. The gases released include nitrogen, carbon dioxide, methane, oxygen and hydrogen sulfide. Hydrogen sulfide is also known as rotten egg gas, and it makes farts stink!

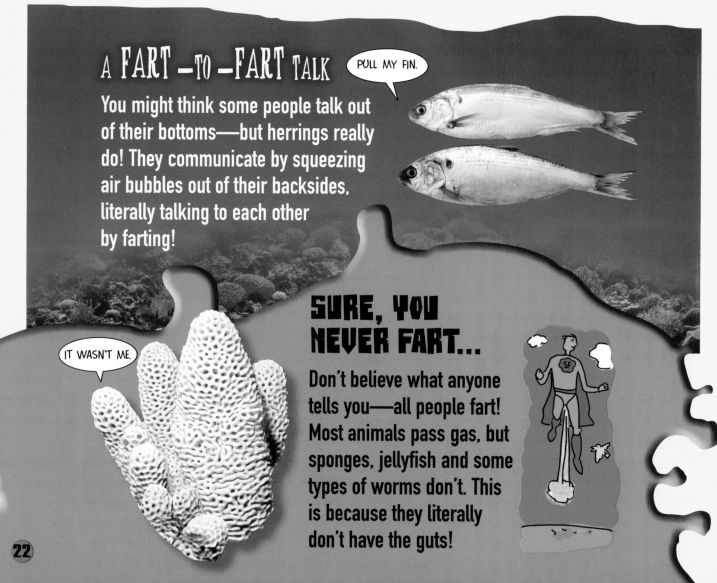

A FART –TO –FART TALK

PULL MY FIN.

You might think some people talk out of their bottoms—but herrings really do! They communicate by squeezing air bubbles out of their backsides, literally talking to each other by farting!

IT WASN'T ME.

SURE, YOU NEVER FART...

Don't believe what anyone tells you—all people fart! Most animals pass gas, but sponges, jellyfish and some types of worms don't. This is because they literally don't have the guts!

size of human bottom bubble

size of whale's bottom bubble relative to whale and diver

BOTTOM BUBBLES

Have you ever farted in the bathtub? Then you'll know what a bottom bubble is! But can you imagine the size of a whale's fart? When a 32-foot (10-meter)-long minke whale lets one rip, it's huge—a big ball of gas nearly 16 feet (5 meters) wide!

An Australian study found that men fart more often than women. On average, men fart 12 times a day, while women fart only 7 times a day.

DOG FART SUIT

Do you own a dog? If so, you might be grateful for this line of research. Pet food manufacturers have created a special suit that measures how smelly dog farts are! They're trying to find which ingredients might reduce the bad odor of doggy flatulence. The outfit captures and measures the different types of gases. The farts are then rated according to their stink factor!

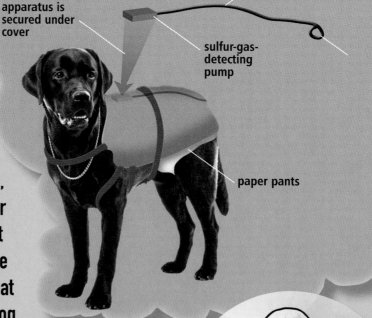

apparatus is secured under cover

connecting tube

sulfur-gas-detecting pump

o-ring

paper pants

FART SUIT FOR HUMANS

I'M JEALOUS...

THAT RATED SEVERE ON THE STINK-O-METER!

FARTY PANTS

I CAN'T CONTAIN MYSELF!

This could be the solution to your dad's problem! Fart-absorbing undies are available in Japan and are selling amazingly well. The product is made of cotton but contains ceramic particles and metal ions. According to the creators, the ceramic absorbs the smell, and the ions decompose it. The company has plans to go global. Add a pair to your Christmas wish list!

GREENHOUSE GAS ALERT

You've heard that carbon dioxide contributes to global warming. But did you know that methane—a gas found in the farts of cows—is an even bigger danger? It's thought that the average cow produces enough methane per year to do as much greenhouse damage as 7,937 pounds (3.6 tonnes) of carbon dioxide. That's more than the average car! Researchers are working on ways to reduce the methane given off by cows and other farm animals. Kangaroos might be the key. Although they eat lots of grass, they don't produce methane.

I'M ECO-FRIENDLY!

CHAPTER 4

NOSES

Different animals have different numbers of scent receptors, or cells in their noses that detect smells. Not surprisingly, dogs have far more scent receptors than humans. But the story doesn't end there. It's also the structure of the brain that matters. The percentage of a dog's brain that analyzes smells is 40 times larger than ours!

Did you ever wonder why you can smell other people's bad breath—but not your own? It's because, after a while, you stop noticing the smells around you. So if you come across a stinky smell, don't block your nose. Put up with it for a while, and eventually you won't notice it as much!

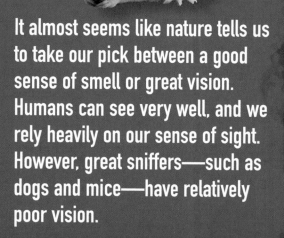

It almost seems like nature tells us to take our pick between a good sense of smell or great vision. Humans can see very well, and we rely heavily on our sense of sight. However, great sniffers—such as dogs and mice—have relatively poor vision.

ANIMAL	TYPES OF SCENT RECEPTORS
Rat	1200
Dog	800
Human	400
Honey bee	160
Fruit fly	70

THE HUMAN NOSE

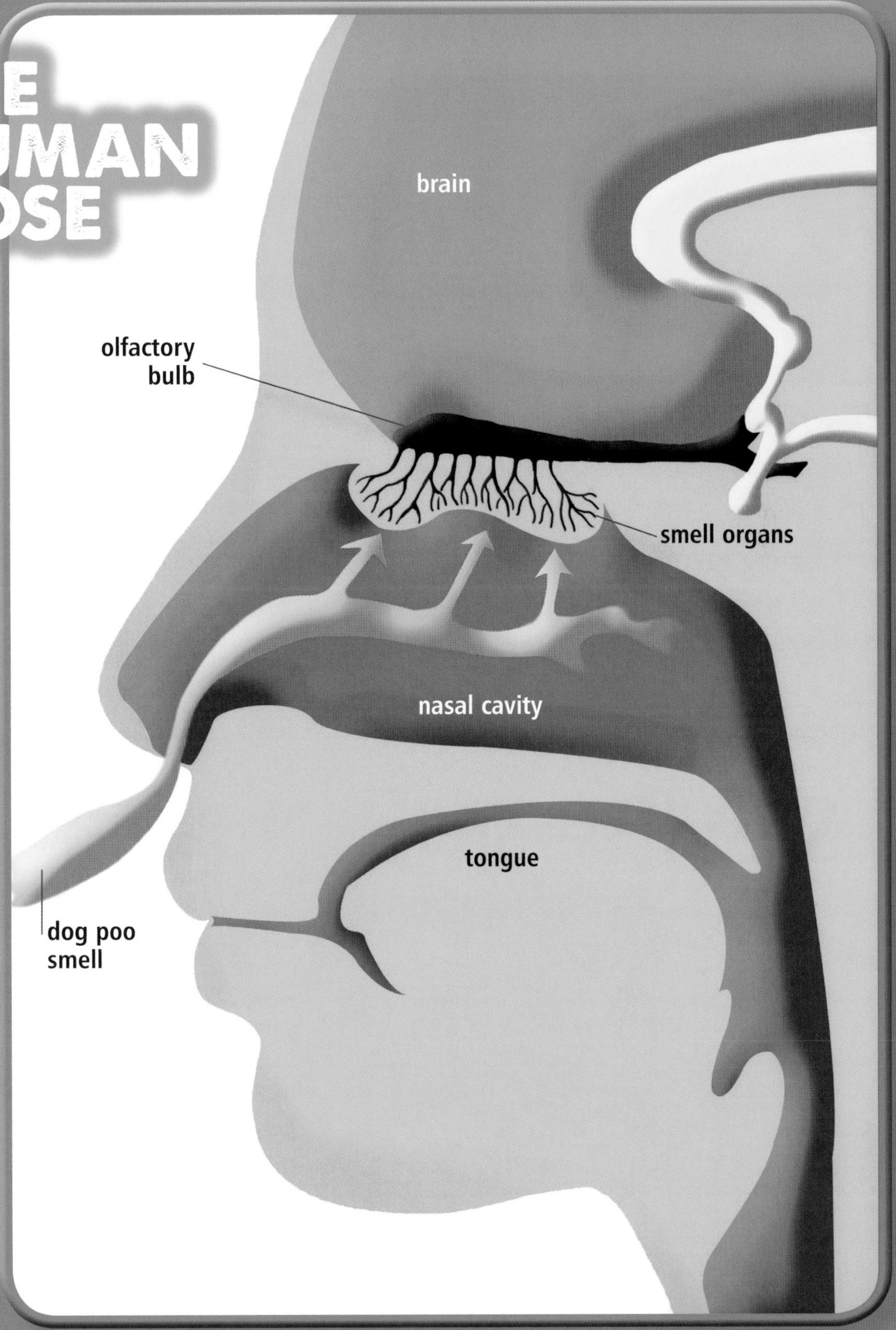

brain

olfactory bulb

smell organs

nasal cavity

tongue

dog poo smell

SNOT

Guess whose nose makes 38 ounces (4 cups) of snot every day? It's yours—and everyone else's! But it's not just so you can gross people out. Mucus traps dust and germs so they don't get inside your body through your nose. When you're sick with a cold, your body produces extra mucus to get rid of the germs. So be grateful and suck it up!

Scientists have found that having lots of snot doesn't just clog up your senses; it changes the way things smell to us.

Dogs have an amazing sense of smell, and it seems we have snot to thank for that! Our canine friends have lots of snot-coated tubes in their noses that may help them to identify individual odors more easily.

SLIME ATTACK!

This ancient, eel-like fish lives at the bottom of the ocean. Despite its simple, tube-like appearance, the hagfish can excrete slime from glands along its body when threatened. It can also absorb nutrients through its skin after burrowing headfirst into its prey!

IT'S CALLED THE BOOGER BLOUSE...

IT'S SNOT FASHION!

How would you like to wear a coat made from snot? Scientists are researching the fibrous slime of the hagfish. They're hoping to produce a super-strong fiber that could be used for clothing. It might even be used to make bulletproof vests!

BEST SNIFFERS

Thanks to their amazing sense of smell, dogs can be trained to sniff for bombs or drugs. They are taught to detect various chemical vapors among lines of luggage. By wiggling each nostril individually, the dog can identify the precise location of the odor they are looking for.

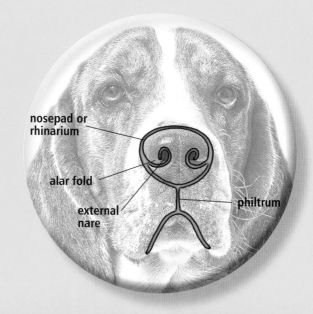

nosepad or rhinarium

alar fold

external nare

philtrum

DR BONYPART PALAENTOLOGIST

THE NOSE KNOWS

A bloodhound's nose contains 40 times the number of scent receptors found in a human nose. That's about 230 million in just one doggy nose! With so many more receptors, dogs need more space in their brain to analyze smells. This part of the brain is only the size of a postage stamp in humans, compared to the size of a handkerchief in dogs. That's not to be sneezed at!

I KNOW YOU FARTED...

Dogs have very efficient ways of detecting smells. Breathing and smelling are two separate functions, so dogs can keep smelling even when they are breathing out! They can even smell continuously for up to 30 breaths!

FRESH ROAD KILL 124 MILES (200 KM) AWAY!

SMELLING IN STEREO

Tube-nosed bats have incredibly agile noses. Their nostrils can function completely independently of each other—this means they even work in stereo! The design of their noses helps them to pinpoint the direction of smells with great accuracy.

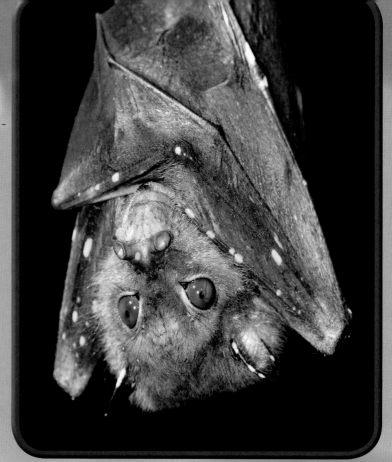

IT'S NO JOKE

Q: Why did the seabird cross the ocean?

A: Because it smelled rotting seaweed! This is the smell that a swarm of krill gives off when it feeds, leading hungry birds right to its location!

DON'T SAY EXTINCTION!

NOSE OF ~~EXT~~DISTINCTION

Tyrannosaurus rex had a better sense of smell than most other predatory dinosaurs. This isn't just because it had such a big nose! A very large part of its brain was dedicated to analyzing smells.

A SNORTER OF A NAME

The pig-nosed turtle is named after its most prominent features— pig-like nostrils at the end of a fleshy snout!

NASALLY CHALLENGED

No nose? No problem! Some animals have found ways to do without. A mosquito smells with its mouth, an earthworm smells with its skin and a butterfly smells with its feet!

THESE FLOWERS STINK...OR IS IT MY FEET?

CHAPTER 5

STINK GLANDS

The skunk is probably the world's best-known stink artist. When frightened, it shoots a potent spray from its anal glands. Anyone who's ever encountered such a smell will never forget it! But the skunk is not alone. There are many other great stinkers too ...

I AM A LEGEND!

TURTLEY RIDICULOUS

NOBODY PLAYS WITH ME...

The eastern snake-necked turtle gets smelly to protect itself. It oozes out an offensive fluid when it feels threatened by predators or when it doesn't want to be handled—not the sort of turtle you'd like to keep as a pet!

DON'T LET THE BED BUGS BITE

Hopefully you'll never come across a bed bug. If you do—block your nose! If a bed bug is disturbed while feeding, it emits a stinky blast to warn other bugs about the danger. Bed bugs also empty their bowels onto their hosts after feeding. Sweet dreams!

THE GIANT AWAKENS!

TAKE THAT!

Some beetles are expert bomb makers. The bombardier beetle mixes two chemicals together from a gland in its bottom, causing a surprisingly loud explosion. It can produce up to 80 explosions in just four minutes! If this isn't enough to scare off any would-be predators, the steam and chemicals that spray out from the beetle's bum will!

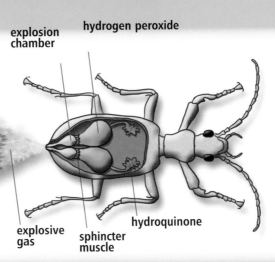

explosion chamber

hydrogen peroxide

explosive gas

sphincter muscle

hydroquinone

Temperatures of over 212 °F (100 °C) are produced in the mixing chamber at the tip of the beetle's abdomen.

KOALAS

Male koalas look like they've been rubbing poo on their chest—but that's not the case! They have a large scent gland that creates the brown stain. They start developing this gland when they are about 12–18 months old. Males rub their chests on trees to mark out their territory.

YOO HOO, I'M HERE!

POSSUMS

Possums like to spread their smell around as a way of alerting other possums to their presence. Pee, poo, goo, you name it— they do it!

WATER RATS

Water rats also use gland secretions to mark their territories. The smell is so strong; it still lingers even after being washed away by high tides!

STINKHORN

The name says it all. The stinkhorn plant is also known as devil's fingers. It has 4–8 reddish arms that are covered with a seriously stinky substance. The stink is designed to attract flies, which land on the plant and help spread the spores.

CORPSE FLOWER

Unfortunately, this stinky flower lives up to its deathly title. The corpse flower, or rafflesia, is the world's largest flower. It can grow up to 3 feet (1 meter) wide. But this is one blossom you wouldn't want in your garden. Rafflesia smell of rotting flesh in an attempt to attract flies that are usually drawn to carcasses.

I FORCED IT...

TASMANIAN DEVIL

You'd want to keep these little devils calm! When stressed, they give off a strong odor from a gland near their bottom. Time for some yoga!

CHAPTER 6

DECAY

Fallen logs and branches take a long time to decay, sometimes even centuries. While they're at it, they make a great home for many different types of plants, bacteria and fungi.

MOLDY GOODNESS

I AM A LIVING CREATURE!

Do you know what makes a piece of bread turn black and green? It's not food coloring—it's mold! Mold spores are less than half the width of a hair, and they are everywhere. Once they land on a piece of bread, they spread out and take over. Mold sounds scary, but it's actually very useful stuff. We use it to flavor foods like blue cheese and in the production of the antibiotic penicillin.

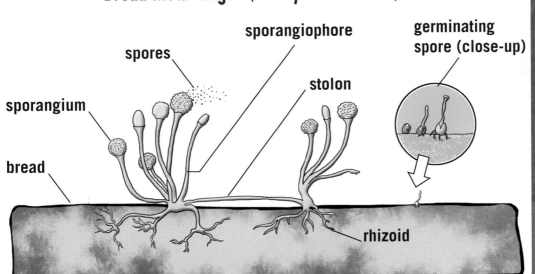

Bread mold fungus (Rhizopus stolonifer)

sporangiophore

spores

germinating spore (close-up)

sporangium

stolon

bread

rhizoid

Did you know there is a fungus that's 1,500 years old? It weighs about 110 tons (100,000 kilograms) and covers over 37 acres (15 hectares) underneath the soil of a forest in the USA.

CHAPTER 7

ROTTING

What do crocodiles, malleefowl and brush turkeys have in common? They bury their eggs in rotting vegetation! Sounds odd, but if you've ever seen a steaming heap of compost, you'll know why. The rotting compost keeps the eggs warm.

NOT QUITE STINKY ENOUGH!

10, 9, 8, 7, 6, 5, 4, 3, 2, 1...
BOOM!

EXPLODING WHALES

Whales have been known to blow up after they die! Their internal organs rot, giving off methane gas. The gas builds up inside the big beast and can reach quite high pressures until one day... BOOM! A man in New Zealand learned this the hard way, cutting into a decomposing whale carcass. He ended up with whale on his face!

WORM FOOD

Dead whales become hosts for several sea creatures. There are even some critters that are so specialized that they can only live in dead whales. *Osedax*, a type of worm, has evolved specifically to eat the fat out of whale bones. The worms tunnel into the bones and make a meal out of something that nothing else can eat!

Anatomy of the *Osedax*

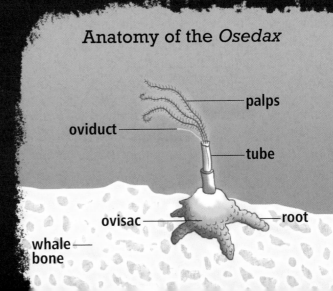

palps

oviduct

tube

ovisac

root

whale bone

CHAPTER 8

CARCASSES & CORPSES

The place where a dead body is located affects how fast it rots. Bodies exposed to air decompose at different speeds than bodies in water. Temperature and humidity also make a difference. Decomposition depends to a large extent on bacteria, so bodies buried underground tend to decompose more slowly than those exposed to air.

GET THEM OFF ME!

CRIME SOLVERS

Did you know that insects can help detectives solve crimes? Dermestid beetles love feasting on corpses. By analyzing the developmental stage of a beetle that is on a dead body, scientists can try to establish how long ago the victim died. The presence of the beetle can even indicate whether a body has been moved after death. Researchers now have evidence that dermestid beetles were even munching on dinosaur carcasses 150 million years ago!

BACK OFF

The smell of death is a powerful warning. Although some animals can eat rotting meat, it would make humans very sick. Biological poisons, terrible tastes and noxious gases are all produced by microbes. They may be revolting, but their stench helps to keep us safe.

Quick TO STINK

The orange-footed scrubfowl starts to rot much more quickly than other birds after death.

TIMELINE OF DECAY

3–7 minutes:	The brain cells start to die.
3 hours:	Rigor mortis begins around this time, and the body stiffens.
24 hours:	Rigor mortis peaks.
3 days:	The body begins to break down due to the action of bacteria. Tissue decomposes, and gases are given off. Insects start to break down the body.
7–23 days:	The body bloats.
24–50 days:	The flesh is removed, and the corpse has a cheesy smell.
51–64 days:	The body is reduced to hair and bone.

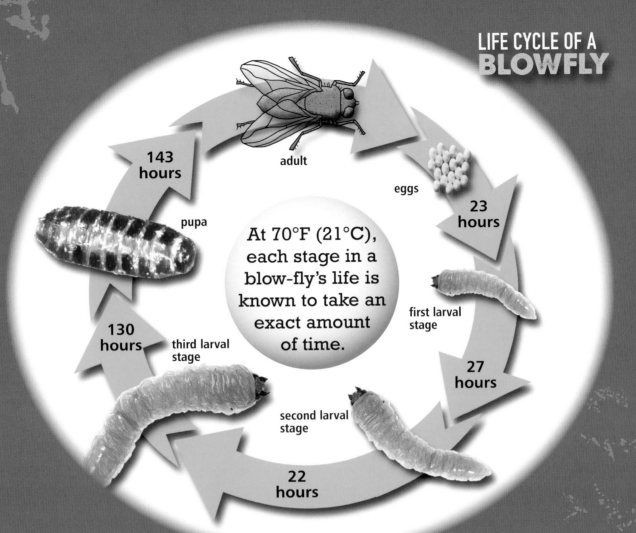

adult

143 hours

pupa

eggs

23 hours

At 70°F (21°C), each stage in a blow-fly's life is known to take an exact amount of time.

first larval stage

130 hours

third larval stage

27 hours

second larval stage

22 hours

HEY! I'M NOT DEAD YET...

Maggots can consume up to 60 percent of a human body in just under seven days! Flies are attracted to all bodies, living and dead, but obviously a dead creature can't swat them away. The flies can settle down and lay eggs uninterrupted. Flies often choose natural body openings for their eggs—such as the mouth, nose, eyes and anus. The larvae quickly move into the body after hatching.

THAT'S STINKY!

GLOSSARY

abdomen	the part of the body that contains the stomach and other organs
analyze	to examine or look at something in detail in order to explain or understand it
anus	the body opening that waste material from the bowel comes out of
carcass	the dead body of an animal
ceramic	something made of clay
constipated	to not be able to empty the bowels easily or regularly; not able to do a poo
defecate	to empty the bowels; to do a poo
disguise	when something changes its appearance so it looks different
eject	to send something out with some force
excrete	to pass waste or poo out of the body
filament	a very thin thread
fossilized	when a prehistoric plant or animal's skeleton or print is preserved in rock
grit	fine, stony or hard particles
harbor	to give shelter to something or to give it a place to hide
herbivore	an animal that only eats plants

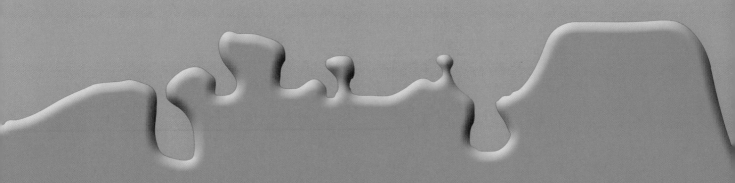

ion	a small particle, such as an atom or group of atoms, that has an electrical charge
krill	a mass of tiny planktonic crustaceans that some whales eat
microbe	a tiny, living creature that can only be seen under a microscope and sometimes carries disease
odor	a smell
offensive	something disgusting or displeasing
parasite	a plant or animal that lives in or on another plant or animal and then feeds on it
secrete	to leak out a substance from the body
sewage	waste from houses and other buildings that is carried away by underground pipes
unappetizing	something that doesn't look or smell good to eat
undigested	when food hasn't been broken down in the stomach and intestines for use by the body
vapor	a cloud of a gas-like substance
vibrant	something lively, bright and exciting

Additional images: